SEEDS

A 50th anniversary collection of 50-word seeds of advice from Redwood Writers

MARA LYNN JOHNSTONE
EDITOR IN CHIEF

Redwood Seeds
Mara Lynn Johnstone, Editor in Chief

First Edition: January 2026

ISBN: 978-1-965617-90-8
Library of Congress Control Number: 2026901313

Cover art and design: Mara Lynn Johnstone
Interior design: Mara Lynn Johnstone

FOREWORD

Mara Lynn Johnstone,
Editor in Chief

While the overarching California Writers' Club was founded in 1909, the Redwood Writers branch came to life in 1975, and at the end of 2025 we celebrated 50 years of "writers helping writers."

There is a lot of collected wisdom here among our many members. We've been helping each other by sharing knowledge for a long time, after all. One of the best things about any kind of writers' club is the fact that other members are on the same page about the writing journey—or possibly a couple pages ahead.

For every club member with a question, there are several others with answers.

When the 50th anniversary rolled around and we put our heads together about how to commemorate it, gathering a selection of the best tips seemed like a fine way to do it.

So here they are: succinct little seeds of advice just ready to sprout, collected in the hopes of helping any other writers who might find them useful.

Perhaps one of those writers is you.

REDWOOD SEEDS

My advice is this: treat all advice like a salad bar. Look at all the options and then try a little of this, a little of that. *Find what tastes good to you*, and go from there. You may need or want to change what you normally eat, and that's okay.

— Stasey Norstrom

If you're hit with the dreaded Writer's Block, try opening a blank document and writing down what the problem is. What can't you figure out? Start listing solutions that WON'T work. Keep going. Eventually you'll find one that will.

— Mara Lynn Johnstone

Always have a notebook handy, in your pocket, backpack, or bedside table, to capture that fleeting flash of inspiration. Whether listening to jazz, overhearing a conversation on the train, or getting up in the middle of the night. Write it down! You may think you'll remember; you won't! Guaranteed you won't.

— Anita Erola

Write to your joy, where you find happiness. Where your curiosity leads you. What inspires you. You have a unique set of skills, experiences, emotions and stories that only you can write in your own voice. Readers will resonate to your truth. Be true to yourself. Your voice matters.

— Rebecca Smith

Don't get too attached to the first draft. The rush of getting those first ideas on paper is just a way to get the bones down. Stay open to changing words, sequence, even the meaning as you examine your work. Let it go where it will!

— Denise Roumbanis

why spare

A certain kind of diction in poems serves to sharpen the blade of silence making us hear it more loudly, more accurately.
(Jorie Graham)

pare away
what isn't poem
examine
what remains

read it   speak it
 note the flow
born of silence
engraving

an echo

— Amrita Skye Blaine

"There's no such thing as great writing. There is only great-rewriting."

(Ernest Hemingway—Paris Review, 1948, winner of Pulitzer, Bronze Star and Nobel honors; five best-selling novels, fifteen stories adapted for movies.)

Rewriting worked for Mr. Hemingway. It now works for me —eleven sales, so far.

—John Lesjack

If you are writing a novel, choose a specific date when your story starts. Print out a calendar from that year, then pay attention to the days of the week for when each plot point happens. Weekday? Weekend? Holiday? Keep your story grounded with the reality of time.

— Linda McCabe

Don't be in a hurry to publish; take the time you need to learn the technical side of your genre. Tap into resources that educate you, encourage you to experiment and build confidence. Mostly, give yourself time and space to allow your true voice to come through in your writing.

— Denise Roumbanis

This may sound simple but at the top of my page I write: GOOD WRITING! KEEP GOING! If I have doubts about what I've written, I simply look up and KEEP GOING! Edits can come later. On to the next chapter!

— Nancy Econome

Tip for Writing Craft:

Get a developmental edit from a professional or, if that's unaffordable, then a successful, published author. It saves time, possibly years. Unpublished writers give good feedback in early stages, but when it comes to readiness for publication, how can they know? Another timesaver: do it after a respectable first draft.

— Pamela Reitman

Don't worry about making it perfect. Get it on the page; perfect can come later.

— anonymous

Let yourself rest. Nature doesn't bloom all year long. Neither can writers. Take fallow time to nourish your imagination.

— Audrey Kalman

Take reasonable pleasure in the work you create but be kind to your editor if you are lucky enough to be assigned with one. The best ones will not impose nor change your subtext. Greater feelings will arrive as the interchange of ideas brings more fruitful results for you both.

— Bill Trzeciak

Creating and promoting your Brand is as important as writing your book. Otherwise, you limit your market to those you already know and those who find you compelling when they meet you.

— Lori Pappas

Read as much as you can, particularly in your chosen genre(s), not so you can copy those who are successful, but so you can see there are multiple approaches that work. This can help you find the confidence you need to embrace your own unique style.

— Denise Roumbanis

Use a critique group. One that knows your agenda with the book. One that doesn't have their own agenda. One with varied genres, ages, and backgrounds to get a world view.

— MP Smith

My writing was deeply influenced from attending the poetry workshop on writing Tanka. Every event became the source of poem, although not a Tanka. I recommend going to Redwood Writers workshops.

—Julie Levine

No matter what you write, make sure you read it aloud—slowly and clearly—before submitting or publishing it. There are flaws your eyes won't catch but your ears will hear.

— Sarah Paris

Life is fluid and fleeting. Enjoy your writing time. Treasure your friends. Do your best. Acclaim may or may not come your way, but your work will matter to those whose hearts you have touched.

— Laura McHale Holland

If you write non-fiction, biographies, or memoirs, protect yourself and your legal rights by establishing an LLC (Limited Liability Company) writing business.

— Elaine Rock

If you're writing a biography of someone who is still alive, make sure you have a lawyer draft an Exclusive Rights Agreement/ Contract, then have the subject(s) sign it before you start interviewing. This can help prevent your subject(s) or their family from interfering or suing you for royalties later.

— Elaine Rock

After completing a draft, let it sit for a while so you can see more clearly where you might want to revise.

— Anna Citrino

Endings are a weak point. Write several different endings—let readers decide. Pick the strongest even if it hurts.

— Roger C. Lubeck

If you're stuck, ask yourself
"What's the craziest thing my
character could do right now?"

— anonymous

There's a reason that some memories move into our heads and lock themselves in the john. They mean something. They impart knowledge or share visions. They serve to remind us of something that we're afraid to lose. Take those memories and use them as vehicles to take you back to that moment. Then use that image as your writing prompt. Populate your memory with new characters. Use it to solve a mystery or answer a question.

— Roy Camarillo

Find subjects that you are passionate about for your writing projects. Don't try chasing trends, because they constantly change. Instead, spend your time and energy on projects that can consume your waking hours and your dreams. That will be time well spent.

— Linda McCabe

You know way more than you give yourself credit for. Just because it feels simple or basic to you does not mean it's easy for everyone. There is always a writer or reader who can gain a new perspective or learn something new through your words, shared experience, or guidance.

— Crissi Langwell

Spending time with other writers is the best! The excitement for writing that we share is so validating and there's so much we can learn from each other. Knowing that others navigate similar challenges and successes keeps my writing journey in perspective and I find it very encouraging.

— Denise Roumbanis

To plot out my story I use a large white board on which I attach Post-it notes describing each scene using a different color for each character. Then I can see how much "screen time" each character occupies in the story. From there I write the first draft.

— Nancy Econome

Historical Fiction:

Immerse yourself in time and place. Learn every facet of life: history, geography, architecture, politics, class distinctions, culture, weather patterns, flora and fauna, food, dress, furniture, heating, plumbing. Read novels, nonfiction, newspapers, magazines—of the time. Research widely before you write, then find the details you need as you go.

— Pamela Reitman

Be very careful with the find/change function. You don't want to change a character's name from Tom to Jonathan, then find the story full of "see you Jonathanorrow," and "the botJonathan of the barrel." There are advanced settings to prevent this.

— anonymous

Have fun! Don't take yourself—or your writing—too seriously.

— Audrey Kalman

Be mindful of your biases when writing a biography. Conduct thorough research using both primary and secondary sources. Be careful about how your perspective influences your historical portrayals. If you're unsure about or missing any information, always inform your readers in the introduction, the story itself, or author notes.

— Elaine Rock

Fall in love with a writing idea.

— anonymous

Learn to remember and write down your dreams. Some stories may come to you whole in your sleep, and others may fill in character backstories, plot holes, or thematic elements. Use the Notes app on your phone when you wake up to write keywords you'll expand on later in the day.

— Bill Trzeciak

Don't discount. It might be better than you think.

— V. Grace Braun

Digital distractions will not help your writing. Put the phone and social media away when it is writing time.

— Crissi Langwell

Write with a group. The camaraderie is essential. Have rules about chatting, but be there for each other's questions and ideas. Respect quiet writing times.

— MP Smith

Don't overthink your story. Start writing and let the story develop.

— Roger C. Lubeck

There is meaning and wisdom beyond our everyday bubble of life. Seek it. Have the wisdom to separate the truth from the lies and the courage to accept it. Write about it.

— Rod Morgan

Save Me from Beheading: How to Write Dangerous Scenes Without Losing Your Readers

1. Replace literal names with archetypes

2. Replace direct quotes with metaphor.

3. Frame it as fiction. Allegory invites readers to interpret rather than react.

4. Assign temptation to your villain—or whatever force—carry the distortion.

5. Favor symbol over citation. Metaphors age better than footnotes. Keep it human. A wink, a joke, or a sidekick's quip lightens the weight.

— Richard E. McCallum

During the editing process, print out your work in progress. Read it aloud. Recognize where you stumble over your words and modify them to have a rhythm and cadence. Even prose can sound poetic if you try.

— Linda McCabe

Lessons Learned:

It's extremely difficult to get published. Literary journals accept only 1-2% of unsolicited submissions. Similar odds for getting an agent. Don't take rejection personally. I endured 600 rejections to get 18 pieces published. But it was worth it! One thing for sure: those who give up don't get published.

— Pamela Reitman

The best way to get better at writing is by writing lots … and the easiest way to write lots is by making it low-stakes. Write little things that don't matter. Explore ideas to come back to later. Take dares. Have FUN with it. Look how much you've written already!

— Mara Lynn Johnstone

Keep bullet point notes of what you want to include in the story next. That way you won't forget, and it can be very satisfying to delete them as you go.

— anonymous

Don't edit your own work. Editing is the polish on your book. You are "too close" to it to be objective or to see simple errors. I've been an editor for 35 years and I hire/ barter/trade/appreciate an editor who can look at my work with fresh eyes.

— MP Smith

Use journal entries for memoir writing.

—Julie Levine

Consistency wins. If you can't write for an hour, write for five minutes. Do it regularly and you'll be surprised how far you go.

— Audrey Kalman

Writing Tip:

Don't be afraid to face your demons. That's where your story's truth breathes. When you write from the shadow that harbors your secrets, your shame, your fears, your characters stop being flat and one-dimensional—they become complex, visceral, and unforgettable.

— Robbi Sommers Bryant

Share your work in the process of developing your manuscript. Redwood Writers does an amazing job in just that essential process.

— Curtis Moran

Listen to advice from others as to how to improve your story. However, also listen to your own instincts. Do not just make changes without understanding and agreeing with the suggestions being made. Sometimes others do not understand your authorial intent.

— Linda McCabe

Shout your good book news from the rooftops! Send a notice (always include links to buy the book) to your alumni group, writers groups and book clubs, and the local libraries. Tell your relatives and neighbors. This is the time to show off what you've been working on.

— MP Smith

First drafts should be written without editing. Internal editors can stifle your creative voice. Scribble on yellow legal pads if it helps. Don't worry about spelling, punctuation, grammar—those will be fixed later. Get your story out and later you can edit with leisure.

— Linda McCabe

Silence the internal critic; have a dialogue with that voice in your head.

Example:
A: I want to write.
B: You have nothing to say.

— Adrian Tiller

If you're starting to feel paralyzed by burnout, this is a critical time to take care of yourself. As you can, set down everything that feels like pressure and take a break. Writing comes easier from a healed mind rather than a struggling one.

— Crissi Langwell

Find your tribe. Don't slave away alone in your freezing cold garret with icy fingers and a guttering candle flame. Get out and meet other writers. Talk with them. Celebrate victories and buoy each other through challenges.

— Audrey Kalman

Every writer's process is different. One will plan out an entire novel before starting, while another will write several different opening scenes before deciding which route to follow. One writes 500 words daily, and another writes 10k in a weekend, then sleeps for a week. There is no wrong way.

— anonymous

Write every day and the blocks will stay away. Every word, phrase, or sentence you begin with may be an avenue to continue traveling along. Save everything, even the worst, until further use. You may even build up a repertoire of varied writing projects to go to when the mood hits.

— Bill Trzeciak

1: Stop thinking
2: Start doing
3: Eat celery between steps 1
and 2

— Guy Cottle

To ensure your writing stays interesting to yourself and your readers, keep a dictionary/ thesaurus handy and consciously apply new words. Word choices need to feel right for who you are and for your style, but it's okay to stretch! This is key to how we grow as writers.

— Denise Roumbanis

Keep submitting. Writing, like baseball, has power hitters and strong pitchers. But to stay in the game you just need to keep coming up to bat. It doesn't matter how many times you strike out before you get your first hit, for you will know then you are a writer.

— Bill Trzeciak

Protect your writing time. Set a block of time aside each day, and keep showing up. I promise you, the words will show up too, with practice.

— Crissi Langwell

Read your work aloud after finishing your draft. You'll hear things that you didn't when reading to yourself.

— Anna Citrino

Write the things you want to read. This can apply to anything: genre, plot, character design, tropes … pick the ones that make you honestly excited to write. If you cater to your own tastes, then you're sure to make something delicious. And other people will likely agree.

— Mara Lynn Johnstone

Have a book party with your critique and writing groups—folks who've read your manuscript. Meet, feed people, discuss your book in a last-ditch effort to find the bugs. Discuss the book by page, chapter, or character. You'll be surprised what bubbles up—likes, dislikes, errors, and wonderful moments.

— MP Smith

Make your own process. If you don't want to get up at 4 a.m. to write for two hours before work, don't. If you don't want to write every day, don't. Find what works for you.

— Audrey Kalman

If you cannot afford to self-publish, hire an editor, or pay for cover art, you can still publish at a free website such as Substack or Medium or one of your own. Just get your work out there enough in your own field of dreams and your readers will come.

— Bill Trzeciak

Write every day at the same time
for a minimum time.

— anonymous

The best way to beat writer's block is to do something else that uses your creative mind. Step away from your writing and go for a nature walk, do some watercolor, create a puzzle, or even just write something that has nothing to do with your current project. Forcing it doesn't work well, but a moment away will help you come back to your writing with a fresh perspective.

— Crissi Langwell

Find a support person or small group of writer friends to encourage you through the publication journey of your book, those who believe in you as a writer and the work you are doing.

— Anna Citrino

Write the rough draft all the way to the end, THEN edit. Don't get caught in the trap of polishing the first chapter before moving on to the second. That's a short route to never reaching the last one. Keep a list of things to fix later, and keep going.

— Mara Lynn Johnstone

When writing becomes ice fishing, as if someone splashed gallons of Wite-Out over familiar territory, your brain a vast expanse of frozen blankness … find a likely spot and start chipping away. Break through into living water. Drop in your line; wait. You just might pull out something alive and wriggling.

— Sher Phillips Gamard

You'll never run out of ideas. The more you write, the easier it is to find inspiration everywhere. If you're worried about the well running dry, don't be! Just spend a little time reading over some fun things, then look around. What can you write about *that thing* right there?

— Mara Lynn Johnstone

Redwood Branch of the California Writers' Club

It was the informal gatherings of a group of writers, including Jack London, poet George Sterling, and Herman Whitaker, that inspired the 1909 formation of the California Writers' Club. The early club's honorary members included Jack London, George Sterling, John Muir, Joaquin Miller, and the first California poet laureate, Ina Coolbrith. In 1975, Redwood Writers was established as the fourth CWC branch, and owes its formation to Helene S. Barnhart of the

Berkeley Branch, who had relocated to the North Bay. She and forty-five charter members founded the Redwood Branch of the CWC. Today the club's membership has passed three hundred members. In 2006, Redwood Writers published its first anthology. This year's volume, Moonshadow, is the thirtieth anthology in the series. Redwood Writers is a non-profit organization whose motto is "writers helping writers." The club's mission is to provide a friendly and inclusive environment in which members may meet and network; to provide professional speakers who will aid in the writing, publishing, and marketing of members' endeavors; and to provide other writing-related opportunities that will further the club members' writing. Members of Redwood Writers enjoy many benefits with their membership. Monthly meetings are open to members and the public, and feature professional speakers with topics that include writing, marketing, publishing, exploring different genres, and more. Every other year, the club holds a day-long writers conference, offering seminars on all areas of writing that are taught by area professionals. Members are also offered opportunities to share their writing and publications at various venues, in contests, in our monthly newsletter, as well as at our club Salons and Writers' Circle. 2025 marks the 50th anniversary of the club's founding. Visit our website at redwoodwriters.org for more information about Redwood Writers.

Presidents of Redwood Writers

The Redwood Branch of the California Writers' Club is indebted to its founders, charter members, board and club members, and volunteers who make the Redwood Writers a success. The Redwood Branch could not have developed into the professional and successful club it is today had it not been for the leadership of our presidents.

2024-26 Crissi Langwell
2022-24 Judy M. Baker
2020-22 Shawn Langwell

2017-20 Roger C. Lubeck
2015-17 Sandy Baker
2013-15 Robbi Sommers Bryant
2012 Elaine Webster
& Robbi Sommers Bryant
2009-12 Linda Loveland Reid
2007-09 Karen Batchelor
2005-07 Linda C. McCabe
2004 Charles Brashear
2003 Carol McConkie
2001-02 Gil Mansergh
2000 Carol McConkie
1999 Dorothy Molyneaux
1997-98 Marvin Steinbock
1992-96 Barb Truax
1990-91 Mary Varley
1988-89 Marion McMurtry
1986-87 Mary Priest

1985 Dave Arnold
1984 Margaret Scariano
1983 Waldo Boyd
1982 Mildred Fish
1981 Alla Crone Hayden
1980 Edward Dolan
1979 Herschel Cozine
1978 Inman Whipple
1977 Natlee Kenoyer
1976 Dianne Kurlfinke
1975 Helene (Schellenberg) Barnhart

Helene S. Barnhart Award

Inspired by the first president of Redwood Writers, the Helene S. Barnhart Award was instituted in 2010 as a way to honor outstanding service to the branch. It is awarded in alternating years of the Jack London Award.

2024 Mara Lynn Johnstone
2024 Les Bernstein
2022 Crissi Langwell
2020 Joelle Burnette
2018 Malena Eljumaily
2016 Robin Moore
2014 Juanita J. Martin

2012 Ana Manwaring
2010 Kate Farrrell

Ina Coolbrith Award

Periodically, the CWC Central Board bestows the Ina Coolbrith Award to honor a member for exemplary service to CWC and/or the Central Board.

2025 Roger C. Lubeck, PhD

Jack London Award

Every other year, CWC branches may nominate a member to receive the Jack London Award for outstanding service to the branch, sponsored by CWC Central. The following members received the Jack London Award for service.

2025 Shawn Langwell
2023 Crissi Langwell
2021 Roger C. Lubeck
2019 Robbi Sommers Bryant
2017 Sandy Baker
2015 Jeane Slone

2013 Linda Loveland Reid
2011 Linda C. McCabe
2009 Karen Batchelor
2007 Catherine Keegan
2005 Mary Rosenthal
2004 Gil Mansergh
2003 Nadenia Newkirk
1998 Barbara Truax
1997 Mary Varley
1995 Mildred Fish
1993 Alla Crone Hayden
1991 Waldo Boyd
1989 Mary Priest
1987 Margaret Scariano
1985 Ruth Irma Walker
1983 Inman Whipple

1981 Pat Patterson
1979 Peggy Ray
1977 Dianne Kurlfinke
1975 Helene (Schellenberg) Barnhart

Fran Claggett-Holland Award

In 2023, the Fran Claggett-Holland Award was instituted to recognize outstanding Redwood Writers members who inspire and live the Club's vision of "Writers Helping Writers."

2025 Robin Gabbert
2024 Linda Loveland-Reid
2023 Fran Claggett-Holland

Redwood Writers Anthologies

Fiction & Memoir

2025 Moonshadow: Tales of Hidden Light
2024 Transitions
2023 One Universe to the Left
2022 On Fire
2021 Remember When
2020 Sunset Sunrise: A Collection of Endings and Beginnings
2019 Endeavor: Stories of Struggle and Perseverance
2018 Redemption: Stories from the Edge

Poetry Only

2025 Just So
2024 One Day
2023 Phases
2022 Crossroads
2021 Beyond Distance
2020 And Yet
2019 Crow: In the Light of Day,
In the Dark of Night
2018 Phoenix: Out of Silence…
and Then
2016 Stolen Light
2014 And the Beats Go On

Combined Prose & Poetry

2017 Sonoma: Stories of a Region and its People
2016 Untold Stories: From the Deep Part of the Well
2015 Journeys: On the Road & Off the Map
2014 Water
2013 Beyond Boundaries
2012 Vintage Voices: Call of the Wild
2011 Vintage Voices: The Sound of a Thousand Leaves
2010 Vintage Voices: Words Poured Out
2009 Vintage Voices: Centi'Anni: May You Live 100 Years

About the Editor

Mara Lynn Johnstone grew up in a house on a hill, the top floor of which was built first. With a lifelong interest in fiction, she has published several books and many short stories.

She is very fond of encouraging others to write out their glorious ideas, and to think of new ones.

She can be found up trees, in bookstores, lost in thought, and at MaraLynnJohnstone.com.

Thank you to everyone who contributed! This book wouldn't exist without you, and your camaraderie enriches the club.

Made in the USA
Coppell, TX
21 February 2026

71864571R10057